WINGS OF MAGIC

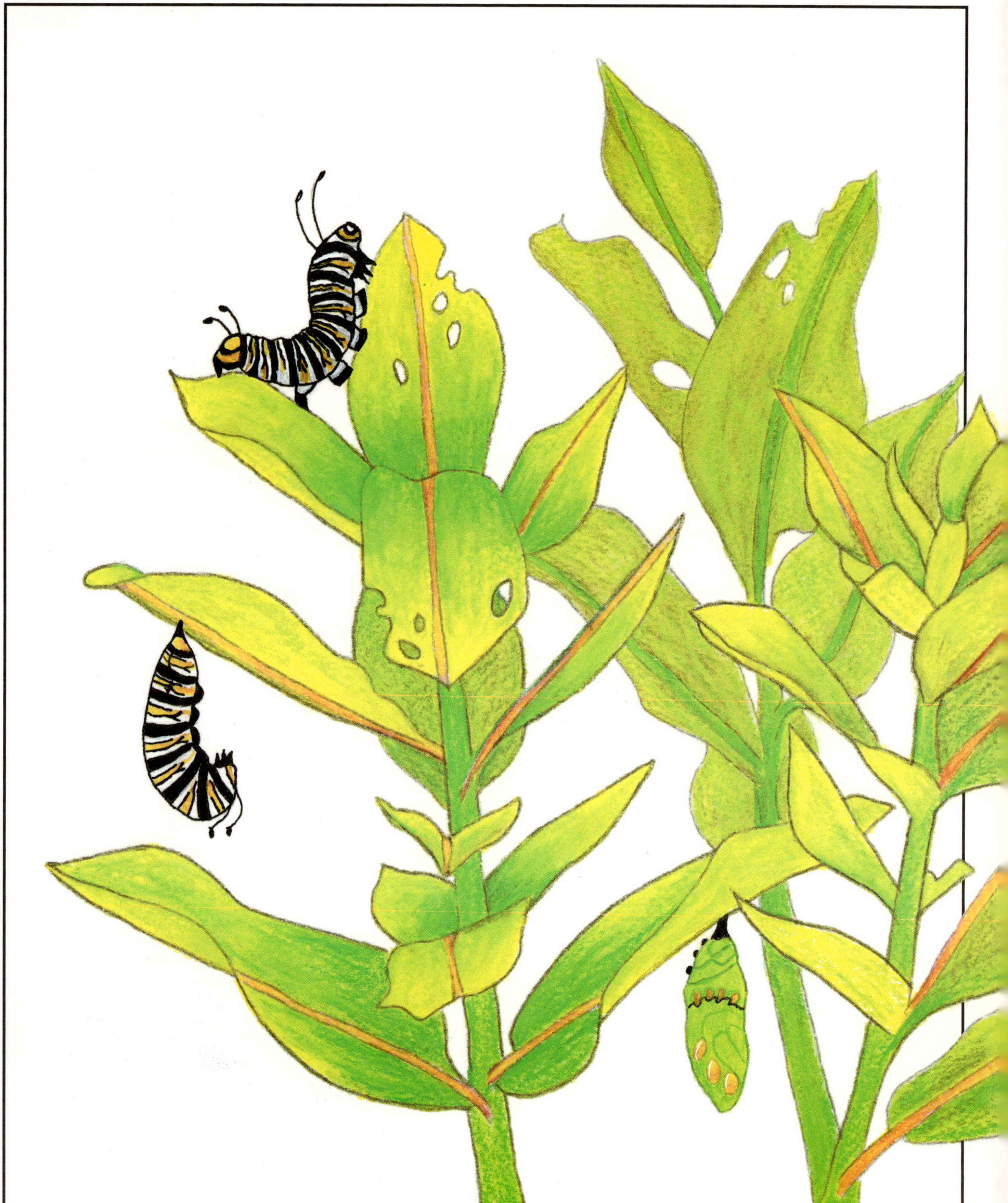

WINGS OF MAGIC

SANDY McCARTNEY EHLERS

published by Ehlers Press
a division of S.M.E. Studio
9449 North Shore Drive
Spicer, Minnesota 56288

copyright © 1992 by Sandy McCartney Ehlers
all rights reserved
second edition

Library of Congress Catalog Card Number 92-90739
Ehlers, Sandy McCartney

<u>WINGS OF MAGIC</u>: words and paintings by Sandy McCartney Ehlers

ISBN: 0-9632737-0-1

printed by
Maracom Corporation
508 Industrial Drive SW
P.O. Box 737
Willmar, Minnesota 56201

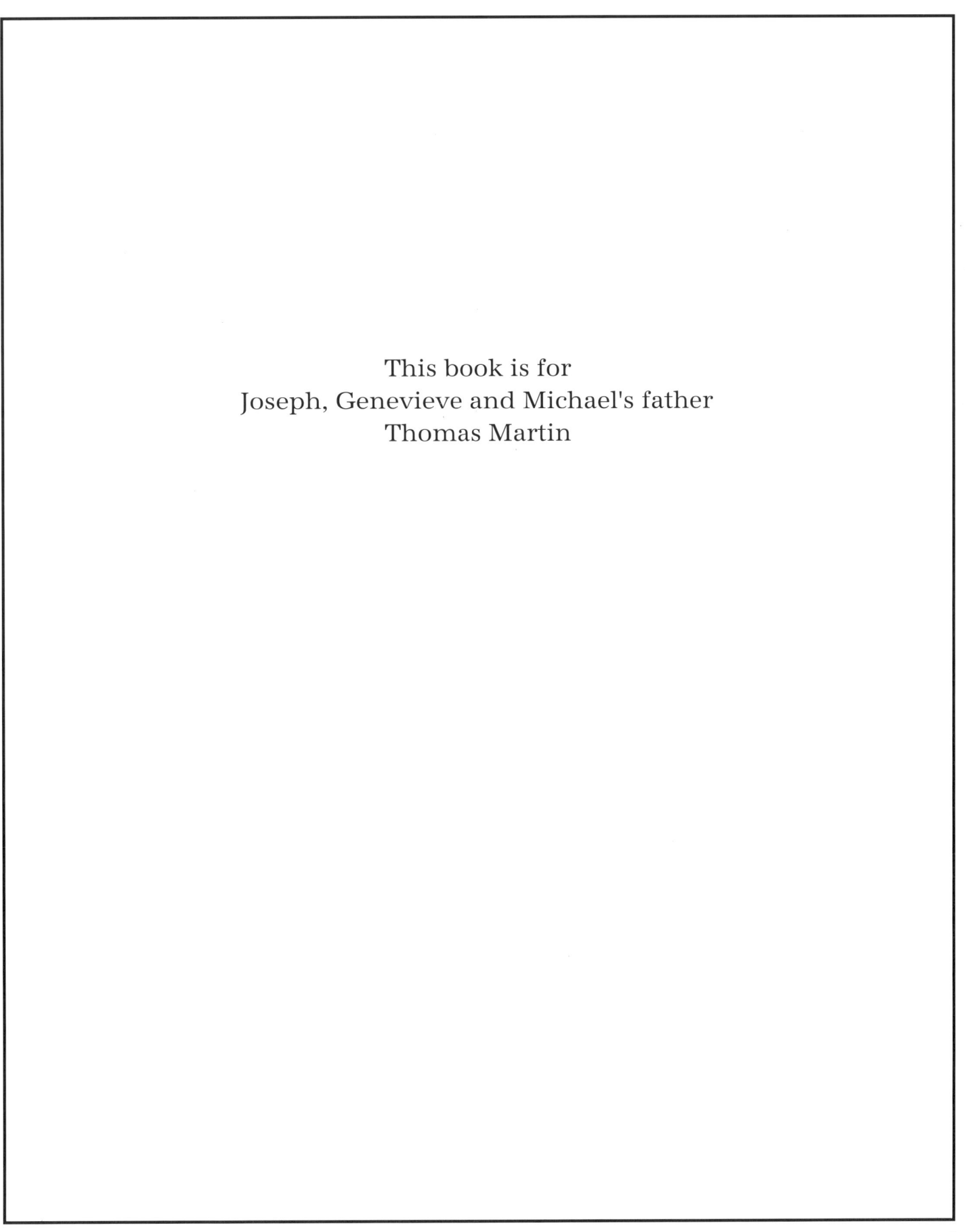

This book is for
Joseph, Genevieve and Michael's father
Thomas Martin

How, I wanted to know, can a lowly black,
white and yellow worm
which crawls about on eight pair of perfect legs

manage to shed its skin five different times

and then, hanging upside down
from its tail,

turn itself into a jade green jewel
decorated with tiny spots of metallic gold?

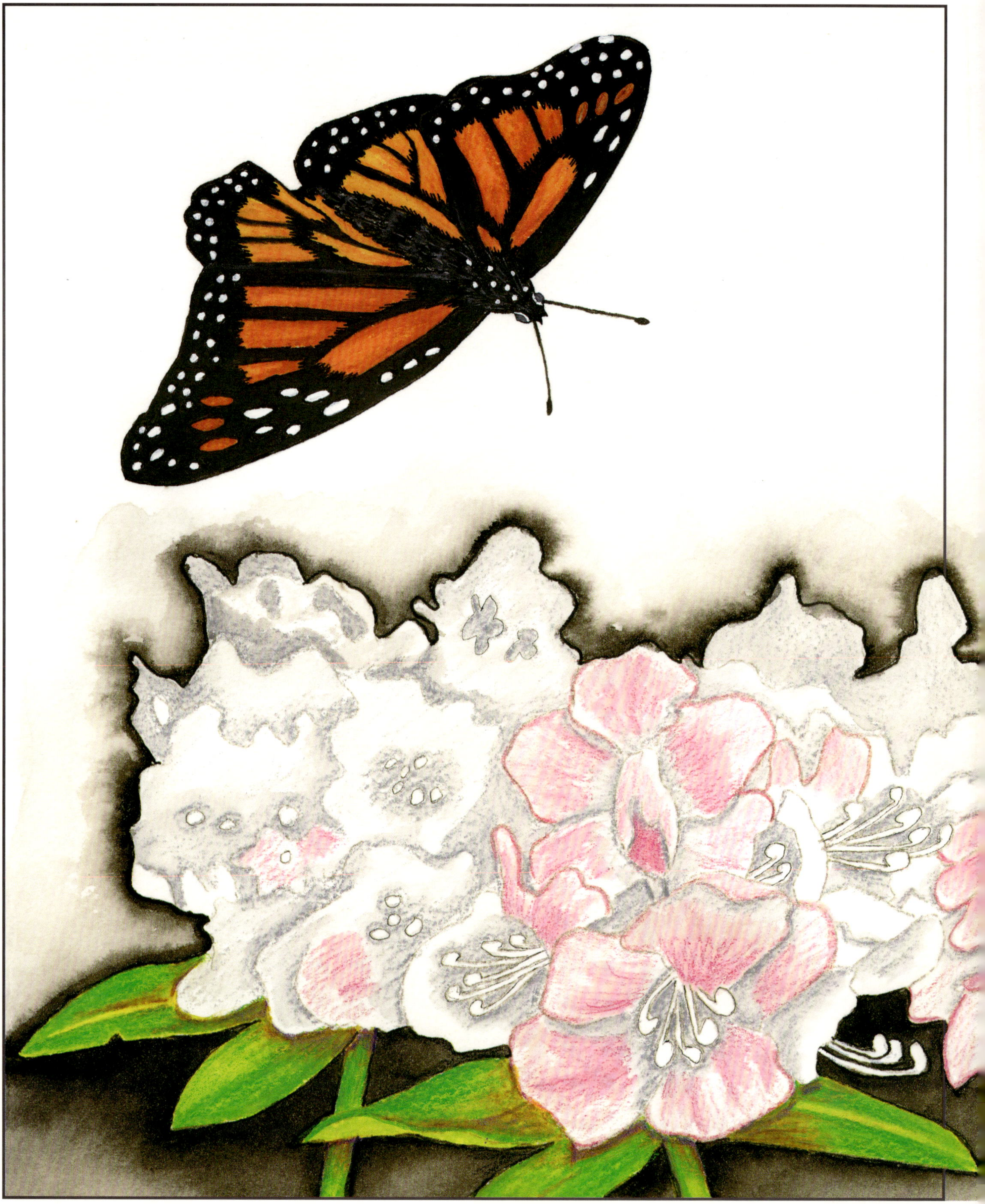

And how does
a beautiful brownish orange butterfly
with black wing margins and veins
plus double rows of tiny white spots

manage to crawl out
of that same little jade house

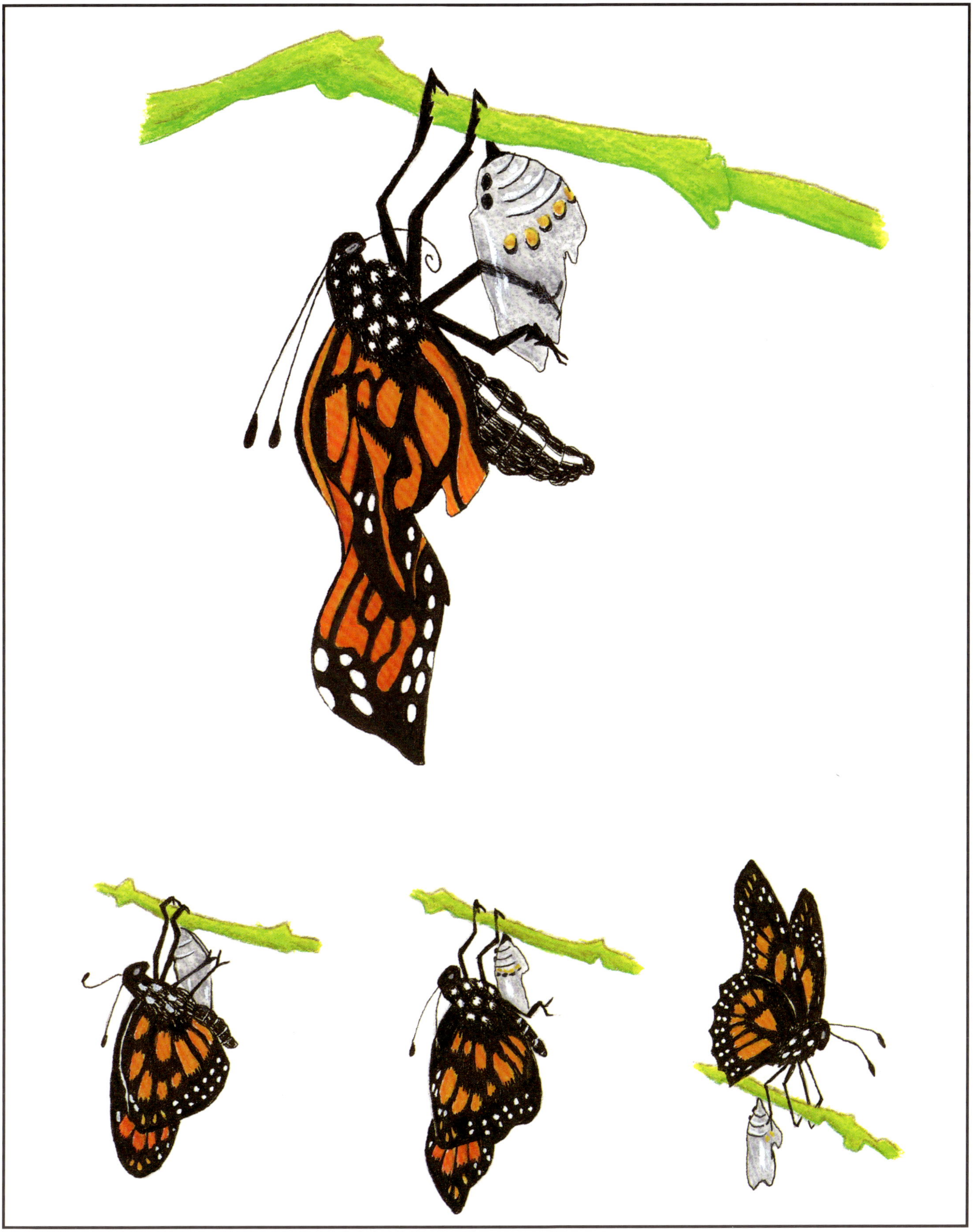

knowing how to raise itself
high in the sky on invisible air waves

where it can sail and dip and soar?

And how can that minute and fragile insect
fly thirty-five hundred miles
to an isolated area in the high mountains of Mexico

where millions of its kind await its arrival,
when it has neither map nor road to follow?

How does it know where to go?
Why does it not get lost?

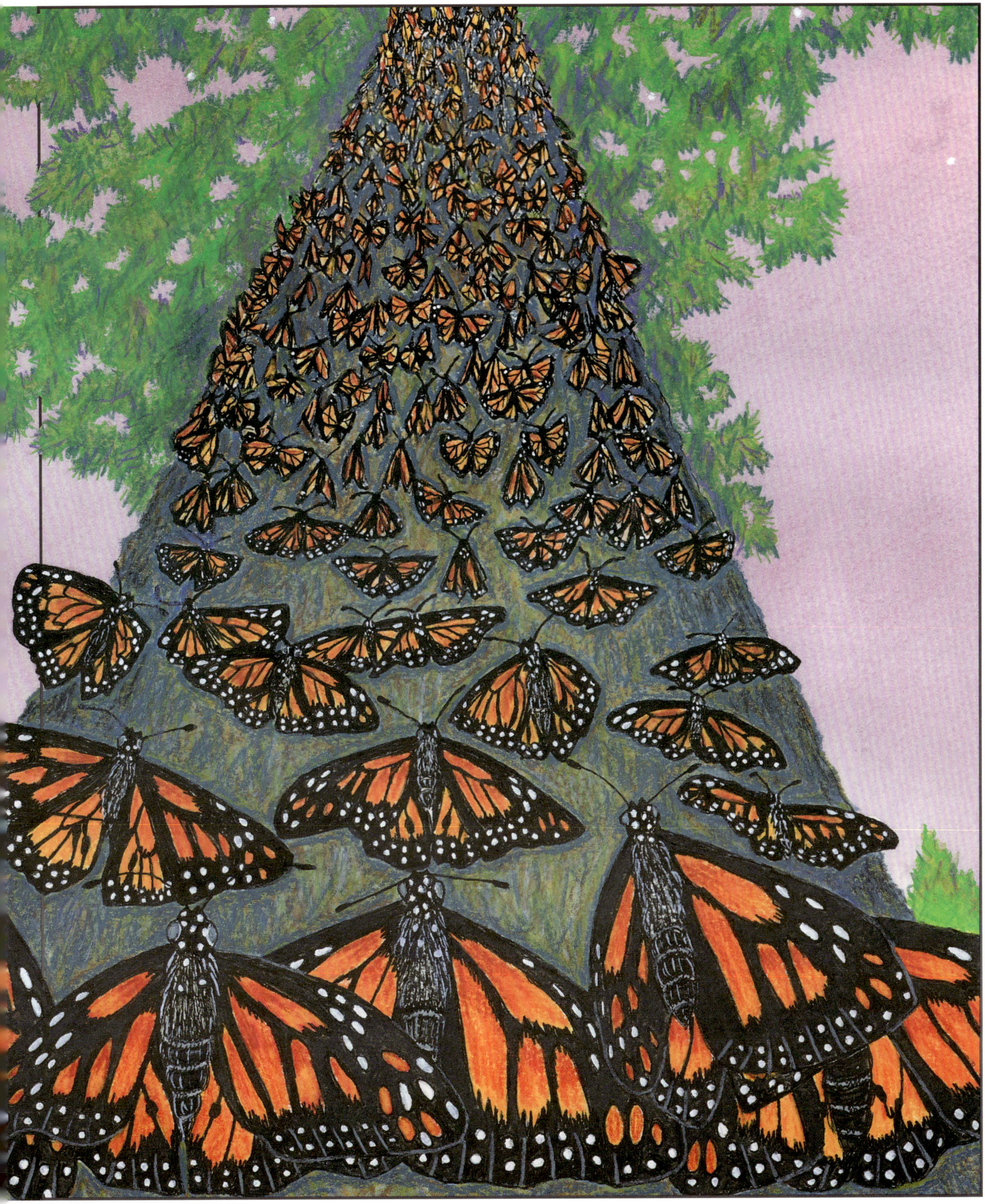

And why does that butterfly

after its time of winter hibernation and mating

realize it must once again return
to the home from which it departed
eight long months ago;

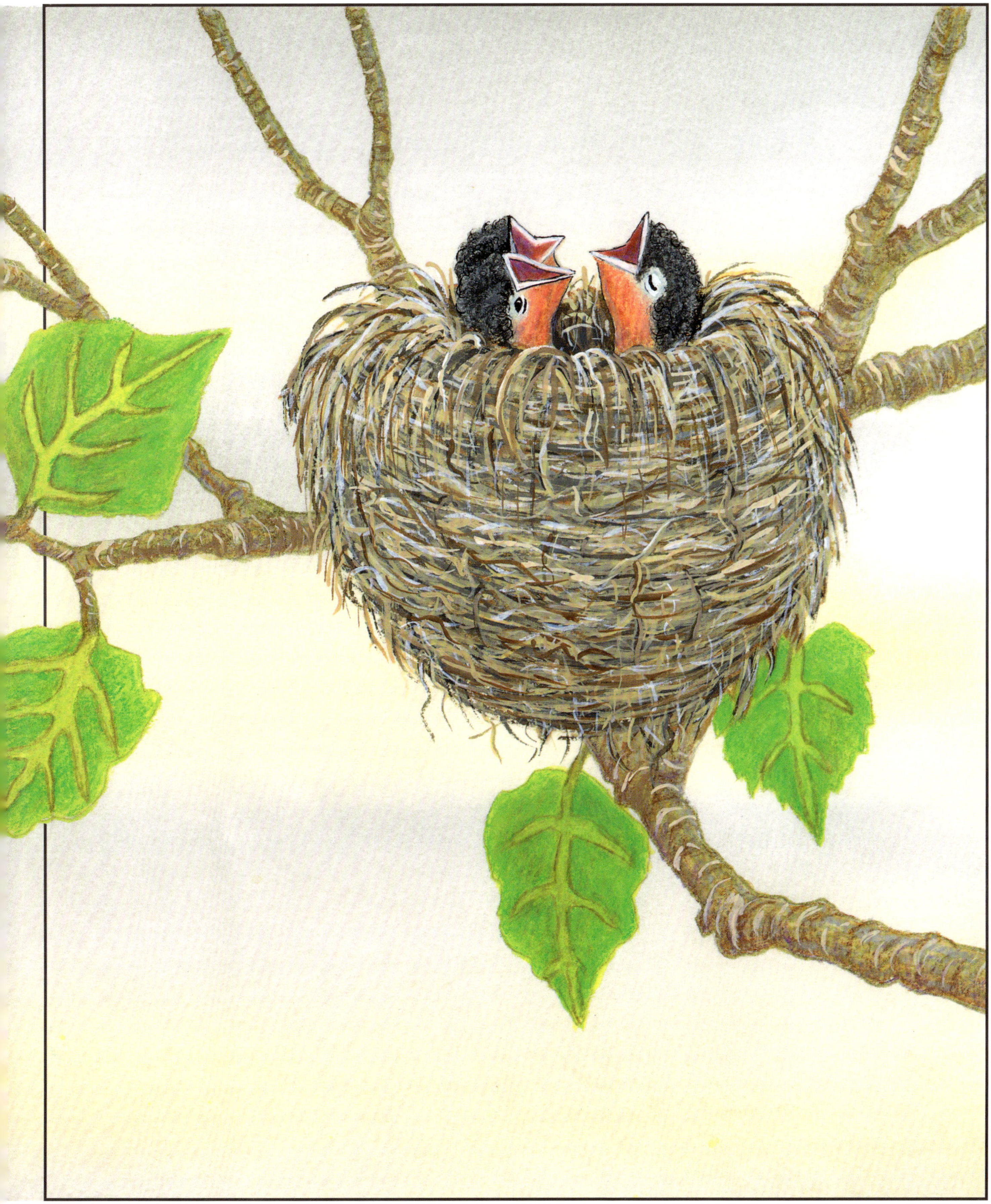

the female laying,
along her journeys way,
four hundred single turban shaped eggs,

25

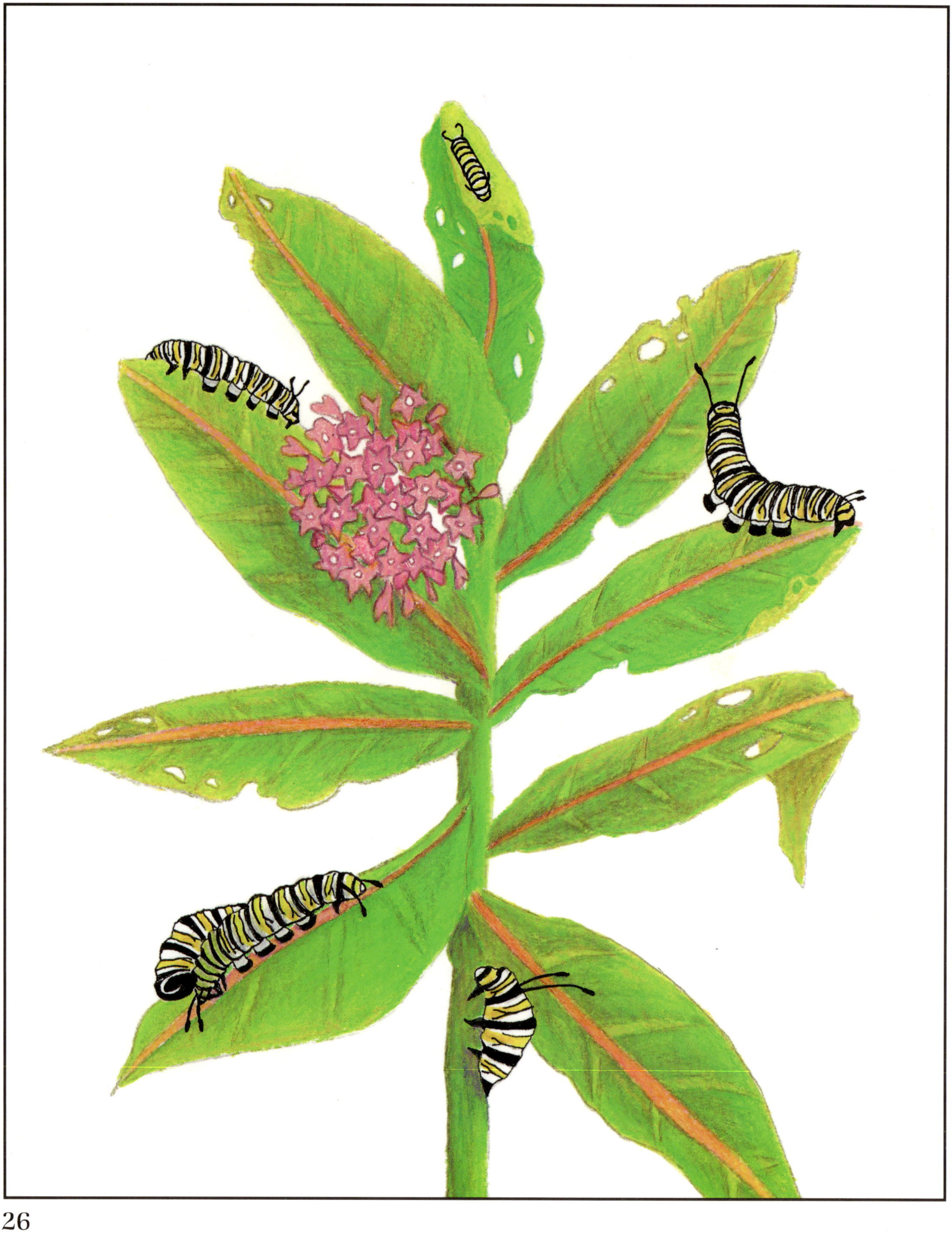

each sheltered upon its own milkweed leaf,
out of which tiny
black, white, and yellow worms will crawl

to begin once again
the transformation from caterpillar
to regal butterfly

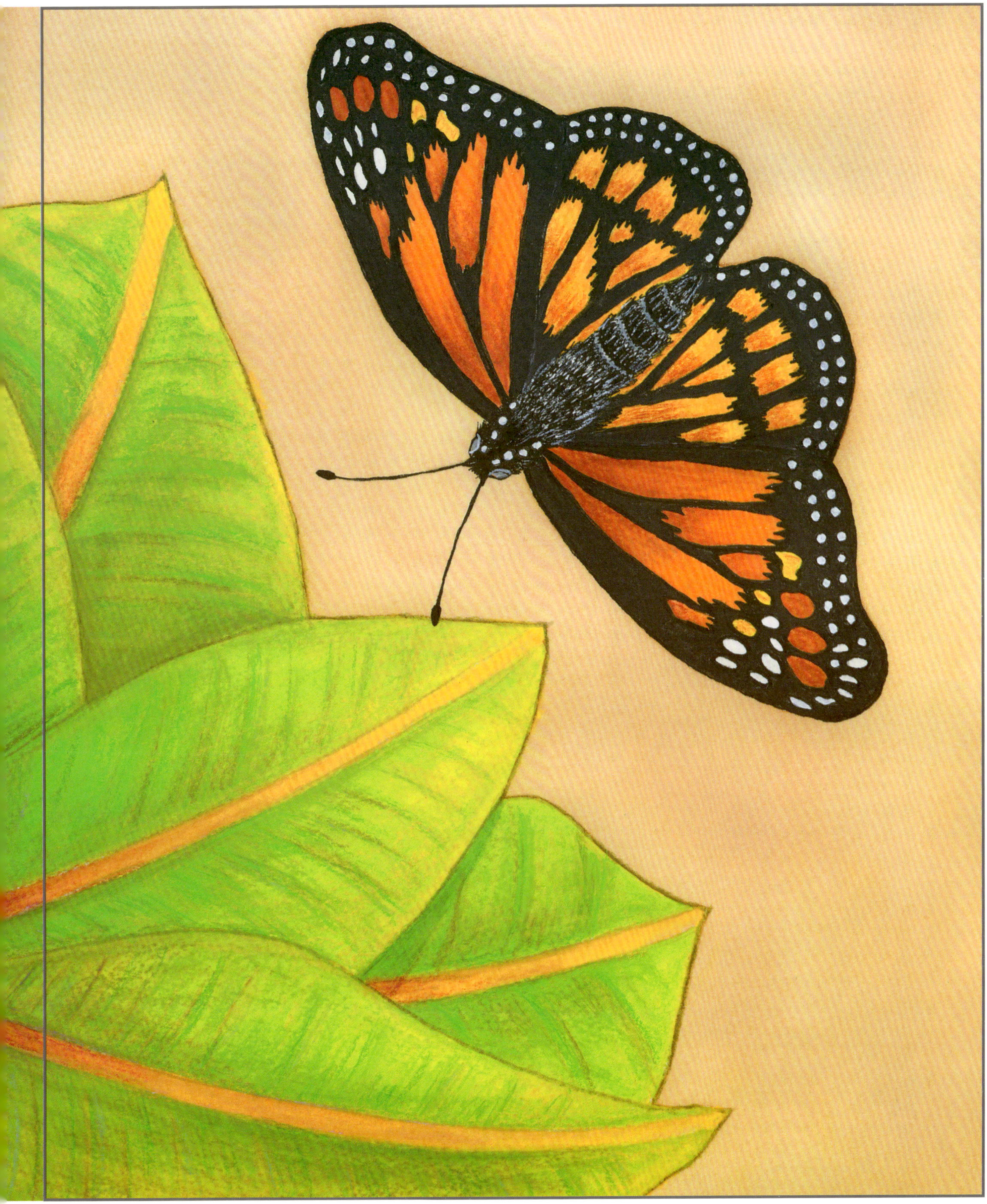

HOW WOULD YOU LIKE TO KNOW SOME MONARCH FACTS?

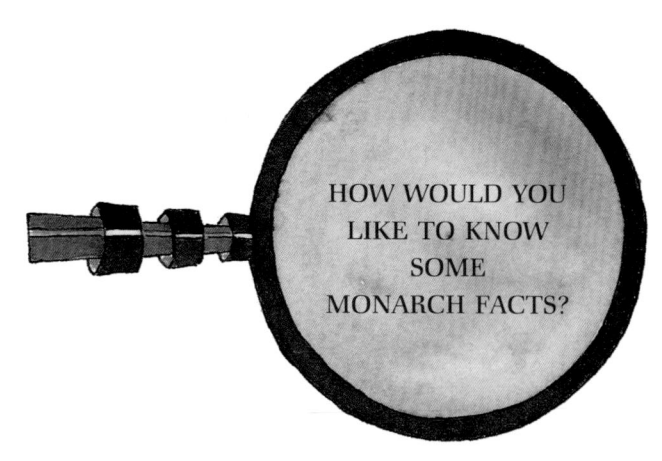

- A newly hatched caterpillar, in its fourteen day life-time, will increase its weight 2,700 times. Were a new-born, six pound baby to grow so rapidly it would weigh 16,200 pounds at two weeks of age.

- Milkweed, the caterpillar's host plant and sole food source, is extremely poisonous. The insect stores the milkweed's death-causing chemicals in its own body to better protect itself from reptiles and birds. Monarch's predators, having once experienced the violent vomiting that results from eating a caterpillar or butterfly, refuse to eat another.

- The chrysalis loses its jade green color after eight days. It turns reddish brown, then dark gray before finally becoming clear, like glass, allowing you to see the butterfly within.

- Ten to twelve days after the caterpillar becomes a chrysalis it begins to jerk, ever so slightly. A few hours after this commences a tiny trap door pops open, freeing the imprisoned butterfly.

- The monarch begins immediately to pump a blood-like substance into its soft, wrinkled wings, causing them to uncurl and expand.

- Monarch wing drying can take many hours when it is damp and cold. If, however, it is warm and dry, the wings become solid and crisp in minutes and the insect is ready to fly.

- Monarchs that hatch in June, July and August have a four to five week life-span and become sexually mature three days after emerging from their chrysalis.

- Monarchs that hatch in September have a ten month life-span and are unable to breed before they are six to seven months old.

- September Monarchs eat so much and grow so fat they can do little but doze and sunbathe.

- Monarchs are unable to fly if the thermometer drops below 50° F.

- An individual Monarch is nearly weightless. It takes close to eight hundred of them to register a pound of weight.

- In late September, just before the fall nights turn cold, the Monarchs begin to form into migratory clusters.

- Scientists do not totally understand what triggers the Monarch's departure but they are confident the butterflies have been making their southward migratory journey for at least 30,000 years.

- Monarch migratory assemblages become so large that it can take five hours before each insect has passed a given point.

- The Monarchs fly fifty to two hundred feet above the earth, cruising at 12 MPH, though at times of rapid flight they travel 20 MPH. Monarchs reach their top speeds when accidentally riding storm-created air currents.

- Monarchs that hatched in America have consistently appeared in British butterfly counts since the 1800's. They have, as well, strayed to the Canary, the Madeira and the Pitcairn Islands, a straight-line flight of 4,000 miles from the United States coastline. The insects are unable to establish themselves as a butterfly species in such remote locations as milkweed is native to the America's only.

- Monarchs that live west of the Rocky Mountains make their way to Southern California while those that hatch in the Great Lakes area and the eastern seaboard fly toward Mexico.

- East coast Monarchs have been known to migrate to southern Florida; from there they fly directly across the Gulf of Mexico to the Yucatan Peninsula.

- The Monarchs' most famed place of hibernation is in the volcanic mountains that lie west of Mexico City.

- Millions upon millions of Monarchs arrive there in October and November, roosting in the Oraemel Fir Forest, which provides the proper balance of moisture and temperature they must have to survive the winter. During their three to four month period of semi-dormancy, the insects live off the fat they stored prior to making the long southward journey.

- The Monarchs' sole winter activity is drinking water, though they occasionally open and close their wings to better absorb the sun's energy and on especially warm days take short flights.

- Monarchs mate in March. The females, after they are impregnated, leave their winter hideaway and fly northward, one by one.

- The eggs they lay along the way are so small as to be almost invisible. Each green egg becomes transparent prior to the caterpillar's emergence.

- The newly hatched caterpillars' first action is to eat its own egg case.

- The Monarchs which mature in spring instinctively fly northward. This assures the hatching of the next generation, for those butterflies returning from Mexico often die before reaching their birth place.

- The Monarchs which manage to fly full circle often arrive prior to the milkweed's maturation. They can be easily detected because their once bright orange color will have taken on a brownish hue. They can, as well, appear somewhat battered, especially if they have had to fly through a number of spring storms.

- If you want to observe the different stages of the Monarch's life cycle, you need to find a large patch of milkweed. Look for plants that appear chewed upon; that is where you will most likely find living caterpillars and chrysalises.

- You can find milkweed growing in sunny areas along the sides of highways and country roads. In cities, milkweed is usually found in expressway ditches that border river and coastline drives.

FORE LEGS
PROBOSCIS
HIND LEGS
COMPOUND EYE
HEAD
THORAX
ANTENNA
ABDOMEN
HIND WING
FORE WING

- The Monarch's body is made up of three parts: the head, the thorax and the abdomen.

- The head houses a minute brain as well as the insect's feeding tube, called a proboscis. It is similar to a long, hollow straw through which the butterfly draws nectar and water. There are, also, two long antennae on the head, arising from between the Monarch's eyes. These antennae contain the insect's sense and touch organs and some scientists believe they receive sound.

- The Monarch's heart is located in its thorax, which has three segments that bear the butterfly's legs, the soles of which serve as its taste organs. The insect's fore and hind wings are secured to the thorax and are operated by internal muscles that continually adjust their angles and positions so the butterfly can control its flight.

- The Monarch's abdomen contains its stomach, intestines, colon and sex organs. The abdomen also houses an air chamber and has room for extra food storage during migration.